The New York Times

POCKET
MBA
SERIES

D0376449

GOING GLOBAL
25 KEYS TO INTERNATIONAL OPERATIONS

JEFFREY H. BERGSTRAND, PH.D.
University of Notre Dame

Lebhar-Friedman Books
NEW YORK • CHICAGO • LOS ANGELES • LONDON • PARIS • TOKYO

For *The New York Times*
Mike Levitas, Editorial Director, Book Development
Tom Redburn, General Series Editor
Brent Bowers, Series Editor
James Schembari, Series Editor

Lebhar-Friedman Books
425 Park Avenue
New York, NY 10022

Copyright © 2000 *The New York Times*

All rights reserved. No part of this work covered by the copyright
hereon may be reproduced or used in any form or by any means—
graphic, electronic, or mechanical, including photocopying,
recording, taping, or information storage and retrieval systems—
without the written permission of the publisher.

Published by Lebhar-Friedman Books
Lebhar-Friedman Books is a company of Lebhar-Friedman Inc.

Printed in the United States of America

Library of Congress Cataloging-in-Publication Data
Bergstrand, Jeffrey H.
    Going global : 25 keys to international operations /
by Jeff Bergstrand.
      p.   cm.—(The New York Times pocket MBA series ; vol. 10)
    Includes index.
    ISBN 0-86730-779-X (paperback)
    1. International business enterprises—Management—Handbooks,
manuals, etc. I. Title. II. Series.
    HD69.I7 B483   1999
    658'.049—dc21   99-27693
                                                              CIP

DESIGN & PRODUCTION BY MILLER WILLIAMS DESIGN ASSOCIATES

Visit our Web site at lfbooks.com

Volume Discounts

This book makes a great human resources training reference.
Call (212) 756-5240 for information on volume discounts.

INTRODUCTION

LEBHAR-FRIEDMAN BOOKS is proud to present *The New York Times* Pocket MBA Series, 12 invaluable reference volumes that are easily accessible to all businesspersons, from first level managers to the executive suite. The books are written by Ph.D.s who teach in the MBA programs in some of the finest schools in the country. A team of business editors from *The New York Times*— Mike Levitas, Tom Redburn, Brent Bowers, and James Schembari—provided their own expertise to edit a reference series that is beyond compare.

The New York Times Pocket MBA Series offers quick-reference key points learned in top MBA programs. The 25-key structure of each volume presents an unparalleled synopsis of crucial principles of specific areas of business expertise. The unique approach to this series packages academic books for consumers in an easy-to-use trade format that is ideal for the individual businessperson as well as an excellent training reference manual. Be sure to get all 12 titles in the series to complete your own MBA education.

Joseph Mills
Senior Managing Editor
Lebhar-Friedman Books

The New York Times Pocket MBA
Series includes these 12 volumes:

Analyzing Financial Statements

Business Planning

Business Financing

Growing & Managing a Business

Organizing a Company

Forecasting Budgets

Tracking & Controlling Costs

Sales & Marketing

Managing Investment

Going Global

Leadership & Vision

The Board of Directors

25 KEYS TO INTERNATIONAL OPERATIONS

CONTENTS

Think globally

The first key to an international operation is to think globally. When asked his citizenship, the Rev. Ted Hesburgh, former president of the University of Notre Dame, typically responds "I'm a citizen of the world." Yet few U.S. business people would respond similarly.

Thinking as a global citizen is a necessary first step toward "going global." For example, Europeans do not think twice about crossing national boundaries for vacation or business. Younger generations think of themselves as Europeans, rather than as Germans or Dutch. We have even entered the "Age of the Euro"—a single European currency. Yet the typical American can often appear like a child to foreigners: naive, unworldly, and even ill-mannered.

Rather than bristling at this accusation, consider a rational explanation for it. The United States is a very large country in terms of population, land and its machinery to produce goods and services.

Where there is no vision, the people perish.

Proverbs, The Holy Bible

Large countries tend to be self-sufficient, both in producing and consuming their own products. Due to this self-sufficiency, the United States has long had little need to transact with other countries, either by exporting goods to them or importing products from them. A consequence is that the average U.S. business person has had little need to learn foreign customs and business practices and, when traveling abroad, is often unaware and sometimes insensitive to the culture and habits of the host country. Such individuals are considered ethnocentric.

Instead, when traveling to a foreign country, you should consider that country as your host. For instance, suppose you went to a business colleague's home for dinner for the first time. You would not show up sloppily dressed and ill-mannered. Similarly, when traveling abroad, one should be as polite and courteous as meeting a girlfriend's or boyfriend's parents for the first time. A useful way to display courtesy is making an effort to use the customs and to speak the native language of the host country. Consider your own experiences meeting with a foreigner for the first time. An effort by the individual to speak English is an ice-breaking experience and reduces tension. Natural barriers are diminished with small efforts of courtesy.

Most businesses going global generally begin international operations in a foreign major city. In most cases, English is the language of international business, making it easier for Americans to initiate foreign operations, but the culture still must be learned.

International business
is different

International business involves conducting business transactions with individuals or firms from another country. The nature of these transactions can occur at one of several levels. A business typically goes global first by either importing a consumer good, raw material, intermediate product, or machinery from another country, or exporting it to that country. In this simplest of international transactions, the flow of goods goes one way. More extensive international operations have two-way flows.

An intermediate product, such as an automobile engine, may be exported to Mexico for assembly and re-exported back to the U.S. firm for placement in the final product. That is often called outsourcing. At an even more complex level, a U.S. firm may purchase property and buildings in a foreign country, hire local employees, bring in some U.S. managers, and produce the good in the host country. This is considered direct foreign investment.

Is this inherently different from conducting business transactions with someone from the same country? In many senses, the answer is no. However, learning how to conduct business well internationally involves understanding the key areas of business where national and international transactions differ.

International business differs from national business because of higher transaction costs, such as transportation costs. However, recent data suggest that the average additional cost for shipping a good internationally, including freight and insurance charges, is only 4 to 5 percent of the value of the product. It should come as no surprise that the biggest importers and exporters of products to the United States are Canada and Mexico, because they are close markets as well as large markets.

International business is also different because host governments often impose tariffs and other nontariff barriers to imports. Tariffs are simply taxes on foreign goods entering the host country. To the extent a U.S. firm must compete in a foreign market at the local-currency price (say, pesos) with a local (say, Argentinean) firm, the U.S. firm may need to absorb the tariff, and accept lower profits, to be price-competitive. Foreign governments often impose regulations and safeguards that prevent penetration by foreign imports into the local market, especially in the provision of services. The additional transaction costs of such nontariff barriers is often difficult to quantify. Not surprisingly, studies have shown that international trade is greatest and most profitable between countries with low tariff and nontariff barriers.

The lack of a common language imposes an additional international transaction cost. Indeed, studies of international trade patterns have identified that two countries sharing a common language trade goods considerably more than two countries with different languages, suggesting an additional cost between two countries with different languages. The more English is spoken in the foreign country, the more likely a U.S. international transaction will be profitable.

Another factor is the prevalence of the media in the international market. Television, radio, movies, and newspapers within a country tend to reduce the transaction costs of conducting business nationally, because mass media tends to either alleviate cultural dissimilarities or at least make such dissimilarities better understood. Studies have shown that marketing and distribution efforts tend to be nationally organized. The absence of a worldwide television and print media raises the costs of international transactions to businesses. However, the rapid commercial development of the Internet is providing a medium for U.S. businesses to cross national boundaries at less cost.

Why go global? Exporting your product abroad is an opportunity, not a last resort

There are nearly 200 countries, and U.S. firms export to most of them. In the United States, businesses that have been successful in exporting often produce goods that cannot be produced efficiently abroad, in many cases because the skills or knowledge needed for production are scarce there. Indeed, firms in both countries have opportunities to specialize in exporting goods that are produced with inputs, such as labor and equipment, that are relatively abundant in each country.

One of the main reasons for two countries to trade is fundamentally identical to that for two individuals (or firms) in the same country to trade. As a professor who had once lived on a farm, I am capable of growing vegetables and raising chickens, working on my car, and cooking my own meals. But I have found it is more profitable, given my education and abilities, to teach for a university, earn an income, and spend that income on groceries, car repairs, eating at restau-

**The craft of the merchant
is this: bringing a thing
from where it abounds
to where it is costly.**

**Ralph Waldo Emerson,
"Wealth", the Conduct of Life, 1860**

rants and still have money to save for retirement. Simply put, people can increase their lifetime earning potential by specializing in a particular trade or profession, particularly where they have a natural or acquired advantage, and selling those services for income to purchase goods and services.

Countries are the same way. Much of successful international trade is attributable to countries differing in their natural comparative advantages and each country's firms specializing in such advantages. For instance, China is richly abundant in its supply of labor, but the typical worker has little machinery or modern equipment with which to work relative to the typical U.S. worker. Consequently, China has a comparative advantage in producing and exporting to the United States low-tech goods, such as Nike shoes. By contrast, in the United States the typical worker has much more modern equipment, skills and knowledge than in China. So, the United States has a comparative advantage in producing and exporting to China high-tech goods, such as medical equipment.

During the U.S. Presidential campaigns of the 1990s, voters often heard Ross Perot and Pat Buchanan make the argument that U.S. jobs would flood into Mexico if trade barriers were reduced on goods from Mexico. The argument went: Because the average cost of an hour of labor in manufacturing in Mexico is 10 percent of the average cost of a U.S. hour of labor (both expressed in dollars), U.S. manufacturers would eliminate U.S. jobs, have goods produced in Mexico at 1/10 the cost, and import the goods into the United States.

Such arguments overlooked that Mexico, while abundant in unskilled labor, is relatively poor in skilled labor and machinery per worker (compared to the United States). Following the signing of the North American Free Trade Agreement, or N.A.F.T.A., in the early 1990s, U.S. jobs did not disappear because, while Mexican labor was 1/10 the cost of U.S. labor, the average Mexican worker had 1/10 the skills or machinery of the average U.S. worker and consequently 1/10 the productivity.

The great advantage of international trade is that potentially everyone wins. International trade is not a "zero-sum game." All countries can potentially improve their living standards by producing goods where they have a comparative advantage and exporting them abroad. U.S. firms have a natural comparative advantage in producing high-tech goods and selling these goods in Mexico, where they are relatively cheap, because the U.S. firms can produce such goods efficiently due to the abundance of skills and education.

Mexican firms have a comparative advantage in producing low-tech goods using the relatively less-skilled Mexican workers and selling these goods in the United States, where they are relatively cheap, due to the scarcity of skills and education in Mexico.

Workers also often win when their company exports. Evidence shows that when all other factors influencing earnings are fixed, a U.S. worker in an exporting firm tends to earn a higher income than one in a nonexporting firm. This supports the notion that an exporting firm can be more profitable than a nonexporting firm, affording higher wages.

KEY 4

The more sophisticated the product, the more likely is success abroad

While countries abundant in less skilled labor can profitably export goods, something happens to that labor pool over time. Eventually, the residents of those countries save some of their income and invest it in banks and capital markets. Firms in these countries will borrow the money to invest in new machinery and plants, and people will also borrow to invest in education. These countries, as the world has witnessed in China, Taiwan, the Philippines, and South Korea in the 1970s and 1980s, eventually become more abundant in machinery and skills. How can U.S. firms still compete internationally?

The answer lies in the product cycle of manufactured goods. The most rapid growth in international trade after World War II has been in manufactured products, not agriculture (such as wheat) or raw materials (such as coal). Manufactured products tend to be complex, relative to producing food or extracting raw materials.

Good merchandise finds

a ready buyer.

Plautus, Paeneulus

For instance, the production of a semiconductor involves at least 400 different steps.

Products face stages in life, not unlike people. There is first a period of invention and innovation, followed by a period when the product matures and is copied in varying forms by other firms, and finally a period of increasing obsolescence and replacement by a new product.

In a dynamic world economy, profitable U.S. manufacturing exporters generally are ones with a commitment to research and development, and produce goods at the early stage of the life cycle. Research and development generally leads to inventions and product innovations. As long as U.S. firms maintain a commitment to research and development, they should hold their comparative advantage in technology.

Just as products have life cycles, so do countries. In fact, the life cycle of countries is in terms of standard of living: developing, newly industrializing, and mature economies. This life cycle makes the potential opportunities for a U.S. exporter even more striking. Successful exporters should identify where a country is in its life cycle and shift its export emphasis accordingly. Thus, the exporter has two options: as a foreign economy matures and per capita income rises, the firm can take its product to a less-developed economy and reduce its participation in the present market, or it can upgrade the product it exports to be more suitable to the present, but changing, foreign market.

KEY 5

Why export cars to Japan?

Although the vastly different natural resources, populations, and educational levels of nations give rise to natural comparative trading advantages, the fastest growing area of international trade since World War II, in fact, seems to occur in seemingly identical products. The Ford Motor Company exports the Taurus to Japan, and the United States imports the Honda Accord from Japan. Surely, the minor differences in skills, education, machinery, and research and development levels between the United States and Japan cannot explain how the trading of virtually identical products can be profitable? How can a U.S. automobile manufacturer profitably export cars to Japan?

The answer lies quite simply in people's taste for diversity combined with economies of scale in production. Concerning tastes, just look in your closet. You don't own one type of shirt or blouse; your suits are not identical. Consumers value diversity.

The nature of producing manufactured goods—the bulk of international trade—is quite compatible with diverse tastes. Manufactured goods often require a large fixed cost to establish the production process, or to switch over an existing production plant to a different product. Once this fixed cost is incurred, the additional cost per unit is fairly stable, so that the average cost of producing the good declines with volume.

So Ford can acquire a comparative advantage (that is, a lower average cost) in producing the sport-utility vehicle Explorer and exporting them to Japan at the same time that the Nissan Motor Company can acquire a comparative advantage in producing the Pathfinder. Countries on both sides of an ocean can profitably produce and export virtually identical goods, as long as economies of scale exist in the production process and the size of the combined markets, say, Japan and the United States, are sufficiently large. Profitable exporters of manufactured goods produced with economies of scale should choose large markets with similar tastes to exploit their comparative advantages.

The opportunity to expand sales and profits through exporting a similar manufactured product to a country already producing that good is mind-boggling. Some people have concluded that foreign markets have become saturated now that U.S. exports have jumped from 6 percent of U.S. Gross Domestic Product to 12 percent in the last 30 years, but this is overwhelmingly wrong. With the U.S. economy only 20 percent of the world's G.D.P., modern theories of international trade suggest that potentially 80 percent of U.S. G.D.P. should be exported.

The profitability of U.S. exporting, however, is not

limited to manufacturers. The wave of mergers in the banking industry reflects the presence of fixed costs that can be spread over numerous service transactions. Rapid growth in service industries—such as financial advising, strategic consulting, architecture—allows new and growing firms to exploit foreign markets. Services, once considered nontradable, are traded increasingly across national borders. Services used by businesses are in fact the fastest growing area of international trade. Technological advances in communication have dramatically reduced the costs of trading services, expanding enormously the potential market internationally.

How does a business go global?

The start of a firm in going global may be active or passive. A passive entree into the world economy is where a firm buys your company's product and then exports it. Alternatively, a foreign firm may initiate an inquiry into your product, handle the purchase and shipment abroad, and assume the risks involved with international trade. The U.S. business does not manage the exporting and treats these sales as if they were domestic. Passive exporting is attractive because there are few costs to setting up the foreign sales.

However, this approach passes up numerous opportunities, markets and profits. Moreover, once the product is sold to a domestic exporter or foreign importer, control over servicing of the product, reputation of the brand name, and customer service erode, and could potentially hurt profits in the long run.

Active exporting involves a business either contracting with an export consultant, known as indirect exporting, or handling export sales directly. Either way, the domestic firm still has to identify and then research the markets abroad.

Of course, you don't have to do this alone. There are numerous private and government institutions that help in developing an export business. Most large cities, and increasingly medium-sized cities, have world trade centers. These provide a forum for exporters and importers to meet to exchange contacts, information, and strategies. Large and medium-sized cities around the world have frequent trade shows, with the New York trade show typically in April. There, U.S. exporters can meet foreign business people who attend the shows looking for U.S. products to import.

The U.S. Department of Commerce also provides several services for exporters, including the National Trade Data Bank, which is one of the best sources for finding markets and has information on the types of products imported by various countries.

State governments also support export-oriented businesses, often subsidizing delegations abroad to generate export earnings (and consequently tax revenue).

Once a company makes the decision to export—and whether to export directly or indirectly—the management must do some research to identify an appropriate market. The firm needs to identify the demand for the product in the foreign market, determine the market structure and identify potential local competitors and/or competitors from other countries, cultural factors that might require customizing the company's product or advertising, foreign barriers to entry, and any incentives provided by the U.S. government to support exporting abroad.

A critical concern in going abroad is tailoring the product to the market. Countries vary in per capita income, levels of education, and cultural factors. Market research needs to address whether or how the product needs adaptation to the market. Adaptation may need to be made in branding, labeling, and packaging of the product.

Research foreign markets thoroughly

Market research in a foreign country can be primary or secondary. Primary research entails management collecting data about the foreign market by interviewing potential customers, conducting surveys, and meeting industry representatives. The major benefit of conducting primary market research is that the surveys and interviews can be customized for the potential exporter. The major cost of such research is the considerable time and resources spent collecting the information.

Once a firm has developed experience exporting, the steep fixed costs of customized interviews and surveys can be spread among more markets as the volume of exports increases.

Because primary research is quite costly, a firm just beginning to go global may instead choose secondary research, which is much less expensive and is often actually the best route for new exporters.

Secondary research should first include a broad "macro" survey of economic, political, and cultural factors influencing a foreign economy. Obviously, a healthy economy is an essential element in considering a foreign market. A potential exporter should look for strong growth in the economy alongside a stable (and low) inflation rate. Rapid growth amid rising or high inflation is either a precursor to eventual hyperinflation and economic stagnation or eventual policy tightening by the government and then recession. Moreover, in developing economies, poor economic policies are accompanied often by balance-of-payments instability and ultimately dramatic exchange rate adjustments.

Political factors must be considered as well. Internal political strife or, even worse, civil unrest or war, generally diminish economic growth and aggravate inflation, making the country a poor prospect for profitable export sales (not to mention the additional personal risk to the company's representatives). Profits of companies generally deteriorate in an economy with higher inflation and sluggish growth. In extreme cases, poor government policies accompanied by inflation may lead eventually to a policy change that prevents a foreign firm from bringing profits back home.

A second tier in secondary research is studying international economic and trade statistics. There are several sources that have information on potential markets, including publications of the Organization for Economic Cooperation and Development, International Monetary Fund, and United Nations. The O.E.C.D.'s *Main Economic Indicators* and *Foreign Trade Report* provide detailed monthly data. The I.M.F.'s *International Financial Statistics* and *Direction of Trade Statistics* and the U.N.'s *Statistical Yearbook* are

The most important word in the vocabulary of advertising is TEST. If you pretest your product with consumers, and pretest your advertising, you will do well in the marketplace.

David Ogilvy,
Confessions of an Advertising Man

not as detailed in information, but the range of countries covered is broader. These sources provide extensive data on important demographic and market characteristics of a country and convey a picture of the current economic and business environment. The Commerce Department's *Foreign Economic Trends* and *Overseas*

Business Reports are other useful sources. Many of these data sources are obtained inexpensively in either print or CD-ROM format.

A third tier in secondary research is paid consultants and direct government assistance. This channel is more expensive than the previous two tiers, in both money and the time involved. International trade consultants specialize in helping firms new to exporting negotiate the web of export (and import) arrangements, financing techniques, shipping factors, foreign government regulations, and customs issues. The Commerce Department's district offices provide counseling to exporters. Each of the 68 district and branch offices across the United States and Puerto Rico offers trade advice; district offices have a staff of trade specialists (each handling a group of foreign countries), and branch offices have at least one specialist who provides advice.

Export indirectly at first

The fixed costs of entering a foreign country to sell a product, especially a manufactured product that needs to be advertised and distributed, are not trivial. A U.S. company that is new to global business and averse to the risks and costs of setting up an extensive export effort should consider exporting indirectly at first. Indirect exporting employs an intermediary for locating buyers in a foreign market, coordinating shipping and distribution of the product, and insuring payment in U.S. dollars. Indirect exporting can occur in various ways, including the use of commission agents, export management companies, or export merchants.

The most common intermediary used by a U.S. exporter is an export management company, sometimes called an export trading company. An export management company represents several U.S. firms in various foreign markets, working on a commission, fee, or retainer plus commission. Often the management firm specializes in a region or industry, developing expertise in establishing distribution channels in various countries and knowledge of the cultures and media network. Such a firm offers virtually immediate access to an export market and the cost of the service is an investment into familiarity in the global market.

One problem in using an export management business is that there is often a loss of control of marketing and servicing the product abroad and an inability to develop closer links to the buyers. However, close monitoring of the export management company reduces the risks.

Export merchants purchase products from U.S. business and then sell the products overseas. Because the product is purchased domestically, the firm loses all control over shipping, pricing, distributing, and servicing after the sale. This approach is less expensive than employing an export management company. However, the firm is less involved in going global, and the long-term profit potential may be eroded by losing the proximity to potential customers abroad.

Commission agents identify products for foreign businesses that are interested in importing them. Working on commission, they have incentives to locate the lowest-cost producer of a good or service. These agents also work for foreign government agencies.

Once established,
export directly

Once a U.S. business has developed some expertise in exporting, it should consider exporting directly. The advantages over exporting indirectly include more control over distribution, advertising, and long-term contacts and service. However, such advantages are costly, including the need for additional physical space and personnel to provide the resources devoted to research, customizing, marketing, shipping, insurance, financing, and accounting of the export operations.

To export directly, the company must first research the best markets for its product. After collecting secondary data about the market, the demand for the product needs to be estimated along with how the product should be modified for the foreign market.

This is an important point, because the cost of customizing the product may determine whether the company has any chance to make a profit from exporting in the first place. There may be a major expense if the basic product needs to be re-engineered. The obvious example is the sale of U.S. cars in England because the driving column has to be shifted to the other side of the car. Less obvious are the power requirements of electrical appliances. Countries vary dramatically in electrical standards and the product may need to be modified. Less costly might be the need to re-label or re-package a product that goes abroad. Some colors may be offensive in certain countries. Brand names may be a detriment in other countries.

The direct exporter next needs to consider how the product will be distributed. The use of sales representatives provides the greatest control over distribution and marketing, although potentially at the greatest cost. However, long-run profits may be enhanced if the product is difficult or complex to distribute or market. Sales representatives may be used on a non-exclusive basis or you can hire someone who will represent only your company.

An alternative to using sales representatives is to contract with a foreign distributor. The advantage is that the distribution firm bears the responsibility and costs of handling the product in the foreign market, saving the exporter significant costs in establishing a beachhead in the market. The foreign distributor takes care of identifying buyers, shipping within the foreign country, and servicing (or at least arranging such services in the local country). However, foreign distributors often represent several exporters in a particular industry and this may erode the diligence the distributor can provide to any one client.

An exporter may instead want to develop a direct affiliation with another retailer. Retailers in foreign countries often represent several imported consumer products. Alternatively, several large U.S. retailers have established operations abroad and use their expertise in selling their product.

Foreign sales representatives are another means of going global. A U.S. firm considering a foreign representative should research the representative's business history, scope of products represented and geographic territories, current clients and volume, methods, and knowledge of the market potential for the product. The Commerce Department provides counseling to U.S. firms negotiating agreements with foreign representatives. An agreement with a foreign representative might preclude representing competitors, but insist on confidentiality and clarify how much responsibility the representative will have.

KEY 10

Gain familiarity with U.S. export regulations and tax incentives

Getting to know foreign markets is complicated enough, but exporters also have to know all the U.S. trade rules, too.

Very simply, all export business must be licensed by the U.S. Government. The main reason for this is national security. Because many businesses in the United States produce high-technology goods that may unwittingly reveal technological secrets to foreigners, the Government licenses all exports to insure no leakage of vital national information. The second reason concerns foreign policy. Certain countries, notably, Cuba and Iraq, are sanctioned by the Federal Government due to political considerations.

Export licenses fall under two categories in the United States: a general license and an individually validated license. The destination country and the Export Control Commodity Number of the product, which is assigned by the Commerce Department, determine which license is needed.

The department's Exporter Counseling Division can help determine which type of license is needed.

A general license for exporting is fairly easy to obtain. However, even with a general license, some exporters may need to file a Destination Control Statement. This statement insures that the export is not diverted to any unauthorized destinations. Over certain values, the exporter also needs to file a Shipper's Export Declaration with the Commerce Department. This declaration helps the Bureau of the Census monitor the volume and destinations of exports.

An individually validated license requires an Application for Export License. An individually validated license is a specific authorization from the Federal Government for a business to export a particular product to a particular country for a specific transaction or time period. If approved, a firm receives a Validated Export License, which includes an authorization number that must be included in the Shipper's Export Declaration.

Rules for individually validated licenses are, of course, more complicated. The Commerce Department's Bureau of Export Administration provides useful counseling on completing these licenses.

The exporter must also become familiar with the import regulations of foreign governments. Tariffs, safeguard regulations, certificates of inspection, and health certifications are just some of the regulations that may have to be met by a U.S. exporter. We address these later in Key 14.

A related matter is tax preferences allowed to exporters by the Federal Government. U.S. businesses can form Foreign Sales Corporations. A business with an F.S.C. can have up to 15 percent of its export income exempted from Federal corporate profit taxes. Export management companies can aid in setting up such a corporation with fairly low costs. An F.S.C. needs to be set up in a qualified host country; most are incorporated in the U.S. Virgin Islands or in Guam to minimize the withholding of taxes.

Understand the costs of
transporting goods abroad

A business can profit more from exporting or importing goods when it understands the additional costs related to shipping internationally. In the case of tangible products, such as a manufactured item, exporting a good involves packaging it, labeling the shipment, preparing documentation, arranging the freight transportation, and insuring the shipment. In quoting a price for selling products abroad, the exporter should be very careful about the terms of the international sale. The new exporter may incur a severe loss in profits when unfamiliar with the delivery terms. Some typical terms in international trade are:

◆ EXW or Ex Works: the price quoted includes the good at the point of origin (say, the warehouse).

◆ F.A.S. or Free Alongside Ship: the price quoted includes the good and covers all costs up to the side of the overseas vessel.

◆ F.O.B. or Free On Board: the price quoted includes the good and covers all costs up to and including delivery aboard the overseas vessel.

◆ C.F.R. or Cost and Freight: the price quoted includes the good and covers all costs to a named overseas port, excluding insurance costs. When the shipment is by a mode of transport other than over water, the term is C.P.T. (Carriage Paid To).

◆ C.I.F. or Cost, Insurance, Freight: the price quoted includes the good and covers all costs to an overseas port, including insurance costs. When the shipment is by a mode of transport other than over water, the term is C.I.P. (Carriage and Insurance).

Freight forwarding businesses are generally contracted to complete the shipment of goods internationally. Such firms are familiar with export regulations, documentation, packaging and labeling recommendations, insurance, and payment arrangements. Such businesses take care of customs and delivery.

Four factors needing close scrutiny are potential breakage, the weight of the shipment, possible moisture damage, and potential pilferage. The containerization of most cargo—large containers that go directly onto semi-truck trailers—has reduced damage and lowered the cost. However, materials should be packaged in strong, sealed, and filled containers. Shrink wrapping has become increasingly used to prevent pilferage and moisture damage.

Thorough labeling of the shipment is a must in overseas travel. Freight forwarding businesses (usually by ocean or air) require designation of the origin of the shipment, weight markings, markings of caution, destination port, and any instructions for special handling. Increasingly, companies use "multimodal" transportation firms; such businesses take care of shipping goods from the factory to the final destination.

The expert freight forwarder handles the time-consuming documentation required for export shipments. Documentation for export shipments is extensive, including the following:

◆ Commercial Invoice: This is the invoice from the exporter to the importer and is analogous to that required for domestic shipments.

◆ Bill of Lading: Bills of lading provide contractual information between the seller of the good and the freight forwarder.

◆ Certificate of Origin: With the proliferation of regional preferential trade agreements, certificates of origin have become increasingly important to insure that appropriate import restrictions apply.

◆ Inspection Certificate: For health and other reasons, some countries require inspections from independent agencies and certification on the shipment.

◆ Insurance Certificate: Documentation of insurance for the value of the goods shipped, if the insurance had been purchased.

◆ Export License: A copy of the general export or individually validated export license (whichever is appropriate) must be included.

◆ Shipper's Export Declaration: This form is filed with the U.S. Treasury Department and reflects the exporter's name, weight of the shipment, value of the contents, destination of the shipment, and other information.

◆ Export Packing List: This form lists in detail the material in each package, type of packaging, weight, and measurements of the package. It is used to determine the weight and volume for billing and customs purposes.

Until 1999, the ocean shipping industry largely set rates as a cartel legally. The shipping industry in the United States has largely been immune to antitrust regulations and has been allowed to set prices cooperatively to stay competitive with foreign shippers. The price stability was introduced allegedly to maintain stability of capacity in the industry. However, in 1999 deregulation of the shipping industry has begun, allowing contracts between an exporter (or importer) and a shipper to be determined privately and consequently allowing prices to deviate from published rates. The deregulation in shipping will likely lead to further consolidation in the shipping industry to take advantage of economies of scale, as happened following deregulation of the airline industry.

The benefits of importing

A re the benefits of importing comparable to those from exporting? Yes. Up until recently, the fastest growing component of international trade was the exchange of manufactured goods. However, a good does not enter the United States from abroad without a U.S. firm importing and then distributing the product. Consequently, a distributor can profitably import goods from foreign exporters for similar profit opportunities as a foreign distributor importing a U.S. firm's product.

First, much profitable importing is in manufactured products that use intensively in their production inputs that are relatively scarce in the United States. If a production input is relatively scarce in the United States, it will be relatively expensive and therefore relatively inefficient to produce in the United States. It should come as no surprise that one of the U.S. industries with an enormous share of imports is apparel and textiles. The production of clothes employs unskilled labor intensively. While the United States possesses a large pool of unskilled labor in absolute numbers, our nation's supply of unskilled labor is low relative to trading partners such as China, the Philippines, and Indonesia. In many cases, importing in an industry will be more profitable the less sophisticated the product imported, as the content of unskilled labor embodied in the item will be relatively higher.

However, profitable importing into the United States need not be constrained to low-tech goods. Much international trade between the United States and other similar countries, such as Germany and Japan, is in manufactured goods produced in both countries using similar technologies. When manufacturing firms face large fixed production costs and economies of scale in production, a U.S. importer—such as a car dealership or a boutique retailer—can profitably take advantage of importing the product that is a close substitute for a domestically produced good, and likely earn comparable profits to the domestic competitor.

Much U.S. importing consists of intermediate, rather than final, products. A final good is one that requires little further processing or enhancement before sale to the consumer or another business. In many cases, an importer may find a foreign supplier of a part for which there is a large need in the United States. Similar principles apply to importing intermediate products. Large multinational corporations typically expand into foreign markets to produce an intermediate part that can be produced more efficiently in a country relatively abundant in different factors. The maquiladoras on the Mexican side of the U.S.-Mexican border arose in the 1980s because U.S. firms needed the factories to assemble parts using unskilled labor, and these parts were then re-imported back into the United States.

How does a business begin importing?

The process of going global by importing goods or services mirrors that described earlier for exporting. The start of a U.S. firm in importing may be active or passive. A passive entree into becoming an importer is when a foreign sales representative initiates contact.

For instance, a sales representative of a foreign exporter may inquire about your firm importing a final good for distribution and sales in the United States, or the foreign exporter's primary or intermediate product being used in the firm's production process as an alternative to a domestic supplier. A more active importing strategy involves using the Internet or attending trade shows to search for potential foreign suppliers of final or intermediate products compatible with your business. In more extensive searches, U.S. firms hire independent trade consultants to scour particular geographic regions to find firms with excess capacity that may be interested in exporting their products.

While the U.S. Department of Commerce is a useful source for information for potential exporters, the department does not provide as much advice for potential importers. To a large extent, this decision is motivated by the government trying to stimulate production and jobs at home, with the additional goal of trying to improve the nation's trade balance. However, just as the U.S. government tends to provide support for U.S. exporters, foreign governments actively provide support for U.S. businesses trying to import products from their country. Foreign consulates in the United States provide good assistance to potential U.S. importers of their nations' goods and services. The assistance is typically free.

While once the domain of only large cities, there are now world trade centers in many medium and small cities throughout the United States. These centers provide an arena for potential importers to make contacts and for developing an importing business. Also, importer directories provide excellent sources of potential foreign suppliers and are available at major public libraries.

Once a potential foreign supplier is identified, contact the supplier in writing. The letter should provide some background about your business and the potential compatibility of your firm as an importer of the foreign supplier's product. The correspondence may include a request for the foreign firm's catalog, price lists, and other sales material. Inquiries into compatibility of the foreign product with the U.S. market are important and will show whether the product will "fit" the local market and meet domestic standards (for instance, electrical compatibility or health regulations).

Finally, as with exporting, there needs to be thorough market research. This is potentially less costly than that for an exporter because the market to be researched is your own. Nevertheless, one needs to estimate the market demand for the product, evaluate the potential profits of importing and distributing the new product, and account for the additional costs associated with standardizing it for the local market, transporting the good, and paying any tariffs imposed by U.S. Customs.

KEY 14

How to deal with tariffs . . . and other government barriers to trade

Whether a potential exporter or importer, a business must deal with a customs department—either U.S. Customs (if an importer) or foreign customs (if an exporter). Because both types of firms face customs, we will focus on keys to handling U.S. Customs, since the general procedures for dealing with customs are mirrored in the foreign country for the U.S. exporter.

Most countries apply tariffs to imports. In this country, the U.S. Customs is responsible for collecting tariff revenue on U.S. imports, which are administered variously as duties, taxes, or fees. Beyond collecting tariffs, the U.S. Customs administers certain nontariff barriers, which may include import quotas for certain products, regulations to maintain national health and environmental standards, and trade policies designed to protect U.S. firms and workers from unfair competition by foreign firms.

Tariff rates vary considerably depending upon the

product shipped and the origin of the shipment. On average for the United States, tariff rates are about 4 to 5 percent of the value of the shipment. However, in recent years, the U.S. government has negotiated and passed preferential or free-trade agreements with several countries. Such agreements provide either preferred or no tariffs on imports from designated countries. The North American Free Trade Agreement (N.A.F.T.A.) imposes zero tariffs on most goods exported from Canada and Mexico. The Generalized System of Preferences (G.S.P.) allowed duty-free imports on designated products from several developing countries. The Caribbean Basin Initiative (C.B.I.) allows zero tariffs on certain products from some economies in the Caribbean. The Andean Trade Preference Act (A.T.P.A.) provides duty-free access on certain goods from Bolivia, Colombia, Ecuador, and Peru. The Compact of Free Association (F.A.S.) allows no duties on certain products from the Marshall Islands, Micronesia, and the Republic of Palau. Finally, the U.S.-Israel Free Trade Area Agreement has been in place since 1985.

Goods can only enter the United States by the purchasing firm or a licensed customs broker designated by the importer. Shipping documents must be filed with the director at the port of entry. The document filings are necessary to insure release of the merchandise from the customs service, proper assessment of revenue tariffs, and recording of the value of the shipment for government statistical data. Recently, parts of the documentation process have been automated electronically. Documentation includes an entry manifest, commercial invoice, packing lists, and other documents. Before entering the United States, a surety bond (or cash equivalent posting) is necessary to insure duty payments to the government.

I never invent anything anymore. Everything I do is to meet a law.

Lee Iacocca, Time

Imported merchandise is generally examined by the U.S. Customs Service prior to release. During this examination, the Customs Service determines the value of the shipment and appropriate duties, country of origin (especially for goods coming from countries with which the United States has a preferential trading arrangement), any excess or shortage of quantity in the shipment (in some cases, an allowance is made for deterioration), damage, or illegal materials.

Because tariffs and other importing regulations can be an obstacle and cost for the novice importer, the U.S. government's Small Business Regulatory Enforcement Fairness Act was passed to enhance the regulatory environment for small to medium-sized businesses. Fairness Boards have been created in different regions of the country to help small importers, and information regarding this service can be obtained from the U.S. Customs Service.

KEY 15

When you should produce here . . . and when you should produce there

Going global does not necessarily entail exporting (or importing) a product or service to a foreign country. As globalization has grown, U.S. businesses have found alternative ways of expanding business abroad. Various methods of internationalizing a business include licensing a particular technology, franchising a service, or arranging a joint venture.

The licensing of technology broadly describes the entering of a U.S. firm into a contract with a foreign business whereby a U.S. company's patent, brand name, or copyright is sold to a foreign business in return for a royalty. The royalty—either a lump sum or a flow of payments—generates income for the U.S. firm, without it having to pay for customizing the product for the foreign customer, finding sales and distribution representatives in the foreign market, and shipping the product or service to the foreign country. Additionally, by transferring technology rather than goods, a U.S. business can avoid tariffs and, in many cases, nontariff barriers that would have been imposed on the U.S. firm's exports. Similarly, a U.S. firm might want to import a foreign technology and enter into a license agreement. Hence, the licensing of technology can be an attractive means for the small firm to go global.

There are drawbacks associated with technology licensing. A U.S. firm loses quality control over the product, which still may bear a brand label. Once the technology leaves the U.S. firm, it may be more difficult to maintain proprietary technological information. Also, the technology may someday lead a foreign firm to become a competitor globally in the same market. Firms considering licensing technology abroad should research the host government's licensing laws and enforcement of such laws. Also, the firm should determine the protection provided by the World Trade Organization.

Licensing is not limited to technology. Franchising has been used in service industries to export a firm's knowledge to a foreign country. Brand names of U.S. services—such as McDonalds, Blockbuster, and Hertz—have considerable demand in foreign countries. In franchising, the U.S. headquarters still supports advertising, education, and financial aspects of the firm.

Joint ventures are an alternative means of entering a foreign market without exporting or importing directly. A joint venture between a U.S. and a foreign firm allows a U.S. firm to globalize its market without all the costs of exporting. The foreign partner contributes an understanding about the structure of the local economy, cyclical economic and business considerations, culture of the local economy, and tastes. If the costs of transporting

> **What makes all doctrines plain and clear? About two hundred pounds a year. And that which was proved true before, prove false again? Two hundred more.**

Samuel Johnson

the product are high, a joint venture can lower the costs of producing and shipping a good.

With a joint venture, the U.S. firm may reduce its exposure to expropriation or nationalization by the host government during economically stressful times and may enhance its profitability by having better access to the host country's business policies. The joint venture also may allow each firm to specialize in an aspect of the production process that uses that country's relatively abundant inputs. Joint ventures have been more popular among smaller businesses, largely to avoid the fixed costs of exporting. Joint ventures by U.S. firms tend to outnumber wholly owned subsidiaries of U.S. companies by four to one.

There are drawbacks to joint ventures as well. If the joint venture limits the U.S. firm to participation of less than 50 percent, a loss of managerial influence may erode the quality of the product or service delivered. This could damage the long-run profit potential of the U.S. business, which might have been avoided either by exporting directly or establishing a wholly owned subsidiary. Because government regulations, tax laws, antitrust, and patent laws vary across governments, the U.S. firm needs to seek expert legal advice before entering a joint venture with a foreign partner. The potential costs associated with a joint venture could exceed those of direct exporting. Finally, as with technology licensing, a joint venture can lead to an exchange of proprietary information that might someday create a foreign competitor to the U.S. firm.

Understand the basics of international payment

I n many cases, payments for exports (or imports) are similar to payment for domestic shipments, such as an open account or credit card. Cash in advance is obviously the least risky payment approach for the exporter and is used in some international transactions. However, additional methods of payment exist that are unique to international transactions. These include letters of credit, bills of exchange, and banker's acceptances.

A letter of credit is a means of payment in international trade that dates back hundreds of years. A letter of credit is usually sought by the importer of the goods from a bank (typically, a large or international bank). The bank confirms that the importer has money to cover the payment. The importer's bank then prepares an (irrevocable) letter of credit notifying the exporter's bank that payment (in a pre-specified currency) will be sent to the latter upon receipt and acceptance of the shipment's commercial invoice, bill of lading, and other documents listed earlier. The exporter's bank receives the letter and forwards a copy to the exporting firm, which then compares the letter of credit's specifications for payment to the exporter's invoice and other documents to insure they match. The exporter then proceeds to produce and ship the product in accordance with the letter of credit. Once the shipment is received by the importer, the exporter's bank receives payment from the importer's bank in accordance with the letter. The major advantage of a letter of credit is that once the letter of credit is confirmed by the importer's bank, payment to the exporter's bank is guaranteed.

An alternative payment method common to international transactions is the bill of exchange, or sight (or time) draft. In this method, shipping documents including the commercial invoice are sent to the importer's bank typically via the exporter's bank. Once the shipment arrives in the buyer's country, a sight (or time) draft is prepared based upon the documentation and sent to the exporter's bank. This is a less costly but riskier approach. The potential risk the exporter bears is that, during the period of the shipment, the importer might change his or her mind and refuse to accept the shipment. In this instance, the exporter bears the cost of shipping the goods back home or finding another customer. By contrast, the letter of credit allows the exporter to prevent shipping the goods until he or she matches the letter of credit to the shipping documents before the goods leave port.

In some cases, the exporting company cannot wait for payment until the shipment is received and needs short-term financing to cover labor, materials, and other costs. When a time draft (a draft on the importer's bank payable at a specified future date) is received by the exporter, the exporter may sell the draft at a discount to a bank; this creates a banker's acceptance. The banker's acceptance is then cashed at maturity yielding the face value of the time draft.

The exporter may even sell the account receivable it has on the shipment even prior to being paid. This is called factoring. A factoring house is a firm that purchases either domestic accounts receivable or even foreign accounts receivable at a discount. The factoring house earns the face value of the payment when payment is made by the purchaser on the account receivable.

Another possible method of a U.S. exporter finding short-term financing is forfeiting. If a foreign importer provides promissory notes to the U.S. exporter, then these notes can be sold at a discount by the U.S. exporter. The forfeiting house then collects at maturity the face value of the foreign company's promissory notes.

U.S. firms just going global should reduce the risks of international payment until experience is earned. Those firms would be better off using letters of credit because they are less risky.

KEY 17

Gain familiarity in the basics of foreign exchange

One of the fundamental differences between a national transaction and an international transaction is that one (or perhaps both) of the parties will deal in a foreign currency. Because most nations have their own currencies, an international transaction requires a payment in one of the two countries' currencies. The term foreign exchange typically denotes any currency other than that used in your own country. In most cases, foreign exchange refers to another country's currency. However, the creation of the Euro in 1999 introduced a foreign currency of 11 European nations belonging to the European Monetary System.

The exchange rate between two countries' currencies is the price in U.S. dollars to obtain one unit of foreign currency, or the price that a foreign citizen must pay in his or her own currency to obtain one U.S. dollar. An exchange rate expressed in "American terms" allows the U.S. business manager to value a unit of foreign currency in familiar

Whoever controls the volume of money in any country is absolute master of all industry and commerce.

James Garfield

terms, the U.S. dollar. The British pound sterling (£) is typically expressed in American terms, such as $1.70 (per £). Thus, American terms allow the business person to price foreign currency similar to other U.S. goods.

The phrase "European terms" commonly denotes the reverse: the foreign currency price of one U.S. dollar. For instance, the German mark (DM, for Deutschemark) is typically expressed in DM/US$, for instance, DM1.80 (per U.S. $). Even Japanese yen (¥) are quoted in "European terms," say ¥120 (per $). Note that the term US$ is used to distinguish U.S. dollars from other dollars, such as Canadian dollars (C$), Australian dollars (A$), or Hong Kong dollars (HK$).

The importance of understanding the basics of foreign exchange is that exchange rates are quite volatile and are much more variable during any day or week than the prices of most goods and services produced by U.S. firms. For various reasons, including the breadth and depth of the worldwide foreign exchange market, exchange rates tend to be as volatile as the prices of shares of stock in companies traded on the New York Stock Exchange, often changing as much as 1-2 percent on any given day. During the first half of the 1980s, the U.S. dollar appreciated more than 50 percent against foreign currencies on average and then depreciated somewhat less than 50 percent from 1985 to 1988, with a typical change in a month varying as much as 20 percent relative to the average change.

The prices of foreign currency, exchange rates, are determined like the prices of goods in any market, that is, the supply versus the demand for the currency over time. If you have traveled abroad, you have likely exchanged U.S. dollars for foreign currencies at branches of foreign banks or at hotels; this is the foreign bank-note market. This is the market for exchanging the notes of countries' central banks, such as U.S. Federal Reserve Notes. The spread between the price at which you can buy foreign currency with U.S. dollars versus the price at which you can sell foreign currency for U.S. dollars is large, because this is a retail market.

Since export and import transactions usually employ letters of credit and banks representing the two parties, the exchange of bank drafts takes place in a much larger exchange market. The spot exchange market involves the exchange of currencies in two different currency-denominated bank accounts for delivery within two business days (one business day with Canada). As of the end of the 1990s, on average about $1.5 trillion of currencies were traded daily. This volume of transactions includes spot, forward, futures, and swap transactions (which will be discussed later).

The choice of currency for the payment for the transaction is determined by the two parties to the transaction. Many U.S. exporters demand payment in U.S. dollars, but not all. Much of U.S. imports are paid for with U.S. dollars. But certainly not all of U.S. exports and imports are paid for with U.S. dollars. If a U.S. exporter chooses to accept payment in U.S. dollars, this business is avoiding exchange rate risk, that is, the firm is fully insuring itself against fluctuations in the foreign currency value of the U.S. dollar. Because U.S. exporters record income, expenses, and profits in U.S. dollars, a payment for U.S. exports in U.S. dollars avoids uncertainty in the dollar value of the shipment due to exchange rate fluctuations.

KEY 18

Identify your foreign exchange exposures and risks

A U.S. business is exposed to foreign exchange risk in many different ways. A firm operating in the international arena is potentially exposed to foreign exchange transaction risk, translation risk, and economic risk. Even a U.S. business neither exporting nor importing goods may still be exposed to economic risk.

A U.S. business that exports or imports a product that involves either receipt or payment of foreign currency has an exchange rate transaction exposure. For instance, a U.S. firm exporting a product to a foreign firm using ocean transportation and a letter of credit for payment typically must wait before payment is credited to the exporter's bank. If the sale is invoiced in Japanese yen, the U.S. exporter faces the transaction risk that the Japanese yen will depreciate in terms of U.S. dollars (hence, the exchange rate rise, say, from 115 yen/US$ to 120 yen/US$) while waiting for the deposit to be made to the exporter's bank. This 4 percent depreciation of the Japanese yen may eliminate the U.S. exporter's expected profit on the transaction. Likewise, a U.S. importer awaiting a shipment invoiced in yen faces the transaction risk that the yen appreciates during the period of the shipment.

Even before the U.S. exporter in this transaction is paid, this firm has acquired a foreign exchange translation exposure. A foreign currency translation exposure is created when a U.S. firm acquires either a foreign currency asset or liability on its balance sheet, because U.S. firms report assets and liabilities in U.S. dollars. In the case of the U.S. export invoiced in Japanese yen, the shipment of the merchandise to Japan creates an account receivable denominated in yen for the U.S. exporter. Consequently, the value of the U.S. business's assets fluctuates from day-to-day depending upon the yen/US$ exchange rate, until the payment is made and the yen converted into U.S. dollars in the foreign exchange spot market. Similarly, the value of any U.S. importer's liabilities varies from day-to-day depending upon the yen/US$ exchange rate, until U.S. dollars are sold for Japanese yen and the foreign-currency-denominated payable is removed from the U.S. firm's books.

Foreign exchange economic exposure is much broader than transaction or translation exposure and does not even necessitate an export or import transaction! A U.S. firm is exposed to exchange rate economic risk anytime current or expected future profits are influenced by exchange rate changes. For instance, a U.S. exporter's future sales to a foreign market and consequent profits are reduced if the German mark value of the U.S. dollar rises because this causes the mark price of the U.S. good to increase for German consumers and erodes the competitiveness of the U.S.

exporter. A U.S. importer's future costs and profits are reduced if the German mark value of the U.S. dollar falls because this causes the dollar price of the German product to increase for the U.S. importer and reduces the importer's potential profits. Even if a U.S. firm neither exports nor imports goods from abroad, a U.S. business is exposed to foreign currency economic risk. For example, suppose a U.S. firm produces a good for the U.S. market and the German mark value of the U.S. dollar increases. A competing U.S. firm may import a similar German product more cheaply, lowering its dollar price in the U.S. market, and eroding domestic sales and profits of the first firm.

KEY 19

Know when you're hedging, know when you're speculating

A U.S. business maintaining either an asset or liability in a foreign currency is exposed to translation risk. In the absence of a strategy to shift this risk to another party, the U.S. firm is speculating in foreign exchange because either its assets or liabilities will fluctuate daily in U.S. dollar terms as exchange rates change. The manager of a U.S. business need not absorb the exchange rate risk often associated with international transactions. In most instances, the manager can conduct a financial transaction that shifts the risk of exchange rate changes to another party. This is known as hedging exchange rate risk.

A U.S. firm is considered to be speculating in foreign exchange if it maintains an asset or liability, or has an imminent receipt or payable, denominated in foreign currency. A U.S. exporter can potentially enhance profits from a sale abroad invoiced in French francs if, between the shipment and payment dates, the French franc (FFr) appreciates in value against the U.S. dollar (that is, FFr/US$ falls). A U.S. importer can potentially enhance profits from purchasing a French product invoiced in French francs if, between the shipment and payment dates, the French franc depreciates in value against the U.S. dollar (that is, FFr/US$ rises). Yet in these cases, the U.S. exporter can potentially erode the profits from a sale abroad if the French franc depreciates against the U.S. dollar, and a U.S. importer can potentially erode the profits from purchasing a French good for resale in the United States if the French franc appreciates against the dollar.

However, the U.S. business just going global is advised against speculating in foreign exchange until it has more experience. Exchange rates are quite volatile, changing on average as much as 1 percent a day. The new U.S. exporter or importer should focus initially on the product in which the firm has a comparative advantage and only speculate on foreign exchange markets in time. Large established multinational corporations maintain foreign exchange departments that typically are under the direction of the corporation's treasury department. The accounting departments of such corporations will often determine every month the foreign exchange exposure of the U.S. corporation and tend to hedge much of their foreign currency exposures. These corporations leave speculative gains and profits to professional foreign exchange traders working at the major money-center banks throughout the world.

A U.S. firm hedges its foreign exchange risk by entering another international transaction that basically eliminates any foreign currency exposure in assets or liabilities (or receivables or payables) incurred during the initial business transaction invoiced in a foreign currency. While hedging is safer for the U.S. business new to foreign exchange risk by shifting the risk to another party, hedging does have its costs. By entering a second (usually financial) transaction to hedge, or insulate, the U.S. firm from exchange rate risk, the firm incurs an additional transaction cost. The cost of hedging foreign exchange risk is similar to the insurance premium paid by the exporter to ship a product abroad. Numerous financial instruments and markets exist worldwide that allow U.S. businesses to hedge foreign exchange risk.

Use currency forwards and futures to hedge foreign exchange transaction exposures

The U.S. exporter or importer new to international business should become familiar with the various financial instruments that insure a business from foreign currency risk on transactions invoiced in a foreign currency. Foreign currency forward and futures contracts are the primary financial instruments used in hedging.

A currency forward contract is an agreement between two parties to sell or purchase an agreed amount of foreign currency for U.S. dollars at a specified date in the future (anytime from three days to five years). For instance, a U.S. exporter expecting payment in 90 days of 2 million Brazilian reals (R) may want to contract today to deliver 2 million Brazilian reals for US$1 million in 90 days; the implied forward exchange rate is R2/US$. Although a foreign exchange forward contract can be negotiated for any time period (say, 93 days) and for any amount (say, R2,312,456), the cost of such a customized contract is expensive, and consequently standardized forward contracts (such as 90 days and 180 days) are traded more heavily in world financial markets. The difference between a currency forward contract and a spot contract is that the latter exchanges U.S. dollars for foreign currencies within two business days (one day for Canadian dollars).

Similarly, a U.S. importer expecting to pay R2 million in 90 days to a Brazilian exporter may want to contract today to purchase R2 million for US$ 1.02 million in 90 days. The implied forward exchange rate is R1.96/US$. The difference between the rates is the bid-ask spread, which generates the commissions for the foreign exchange traders.

Foreign exchange forward contracts typically have values of US$1 million or more and are generally used by large multinational corporations due to their extensive and sizable international transactions. Small and medium-sized U.S. firms may use foreign exchange futures contracts instead. A currency futures contract is also an agreement between two parties to exchange two currencies at a specified date in the future. Currency futures contracts differ from forward contracts because the former are standardized in terms of a certain date and time for expiration (in most countries, four expiration dates per year), type of foreign currency, and amount of foreign currency.

For instance, a U.S. exporter expecting delivery of 260,000 Swiss francs (SwF) on June 30 from a Swiss importer may sell today two (standardized) futures contracts for SwF125,000 for delivery on June 16 at a price of $0.67/SwF. A U.S. importer expecting a payment of SwF260,000 on June 30 to a Swiss exporter may purchase two futures contracts for SwF125,00 for purchase on June 16 at a price of $0.68/SwF. Given the standardized nature of futures currency contracts, expiration dates and currency sizes will not match precisely an exporter's or importer's exposure. However, the purchase or sale of the futures contract hedges most of the foreign exchange exposure and at a cost significantly less than that for a comparable forward contract.

In the United States, the International Money Market (I.M.M.) of the Chicago Mercantile Exchange (C.M.E.) provides widely traded markets in currency futures contracts for Canadian dollars, Japanese yen, German marks, British pounds, Swiss francs, and Mexican pesos. The C.M.E. has an excellent web site for learning further about foreign currency futures at www.cme.com.

Uses for foreign currency swaps and options

The U.S. exporter or importer new to international business should become familiar with the various financial instruments that insure a business from foreign currency risk on assets or liabilities denominated in a foreign currency or potential sales or purchases. For instance, a U.S. business that has established an operation overseas may have invested in property or real estate in a foreign country. The foreign real estate fluctuates in value partly due to variation in exchange rates, adding volatility to the value of the firm's assets. This creates foreign currency translation risk. A U.S. firm may want to go global by bidding on a foreign contract, not knowing with certainty for months whether or not a purchase of local materials invoiced in foreign currency will be made. This creates foreign currency economic risk. There are ways to hedge both risks.

A primary instrument for insulating a U.S. firm's dollar-denominated assets or liabilities from foreign exchange risk is currency swaps. For instance, suppose a U.S. firm acquires property in Mexico worth 10 million Mexican pesos. The value of this asset fluctuates in U.S. dollars with the US$/peso exchange rate; if the dollar value of the peso falls, the U.S. firm's assets decline (in US$). One way to hedge this translation risk is to sell 10 million pesos forward one-year for, say, US$1 million. No currencies are exchanged initially with the forward contract.

However, in one year the U.S. firm is obligated to sell 10 million pesos for US$1 million. If the Mexican property has not been sold and the U.S. firm wishes to retain the property and continue the hedge, it can enter a spot-forward swap. The U.S. firm contracts to buy 10 million pesos (selling approximately US$1 million) spot and sell 10 million pesos (buying approximately US$1 million) forward. The out-of-pocket cost of the swap transaction is small, much like an insurance premium. Conducting this transaction annually for this small insurance premium eliminates the firm's foreign currency translation exposure.

Exchange rate economic exposure is more difficult to shift away because it concerns uncertain economic events that may affect expected future profits. For instance, suppose a U.S. business decides to bid on the supply of computer software to the Chinese government for 10 million Chinese renminbi. However, the outcome of the bid will not be known for six months. If the U.S. exporter wins the contract then, the firm faces a foreign currency receivable of 10 million renminbi—with uncertain U.S. dollar value; if the U.S. firm loses the contract, it faces no foreign currency receivable.

A primary instrument for insulating the U.S. firm's uncertain economic exposure is to purchase a currency put option. This option gives the purchaser the right (but not obligation!) to sell 10 million renminbi in six months at a price specified today. If during the six months the renminbi depreciates in value against the dollar (US$/renminbi falls), the U.S. firm exercises the currency option, insuring the U.S. dollar value of the foreign currency receivable. If during the six months the renminbi appreciates in value against the dollar (US$/renminbi rises), then the U.S. firm can simply let the option expire. The cost of the option is fairly low, once again similar to an insurance premium.

KEY 22

Save some money: use "natural" hedges

Although the unprecedented growth of financial derivatives has helped international trade and investment grow, U.S. managers can save some money by using natural hedges. The financial hedging instruments—such as currency forward, futures, swap, and options contracts—just described are considered synthetic hedges. A natural hedge is one where the behavior of fairly efficient markets leads to certain price adjustments that "naturally" protect the U.S. firm from foreign currency exposures.

One of the greatest concerns of the typical U.S. exporter is an appreciation of the U.S. dollar in foreign exchange markets. For instance, suppose a U.S. exporter ships goods to Germany with the sale invoiced in Euros, the new European currency. Suppose during the shipment the U.S. dollar appreciates against the Euro in the foreign exchange market. The appreciation of the dollar implies a depreciation of the Euro (US$/Euro falls). As the US$/Euro exchange rate declines, the U.S. exporter's dollar-denominated revenues and profits decline. As discussed earlier, though, this transaction risk for the U.S. exporter can be hedged by contracting today to sell Euros forward.

However, this appreciation of the U.S. dollar also creates an economic risk for the U.S. exporter. As the dollar appreciates against the Euro (Euro/US$ rises), the Euro price of a U.S. product rises (Euro/U.S. good rises for a given US$/US good), eroding the competitiveness of the U.S. exporter. Because currencies can appreciate or depreciate for prolonged periods, this economic exposure is costly to avoid using synthetic hedges. Yet the U.S. exporter does have a natural hedge, at least over the long run.

The natural hedge here is purchasing power parity. Purchasing power parity refers to the notion that the relative price of two countries' goods in a common currency is constant; thus, the U.S. exporter has a natural hedge against economic risk. Under purchasing power parity, differences in inflation rates between two countries will equal the change in their exchange rate over time. For instance, if U.S. prices rise over time at a 2 percent annual rate and German prices rise over time at a 1 percent annual rate, evidence suggests that the U.S. dollar will depreciate on average about 1 percent against the mark, if the two countries' productivity growth rates are roughly similar. (If German productivity grows faster than U.S. productivity, then the U.S. dollar will likely depreciate even faster than 1 percent.) Even though in the short-run exchange rates are quite volatile for U.S. exporters and importers, such temporary departures from purchasing power parity tend to disappear within 4-5 years on average. Thus, U.S. exporters and importers have potential natural hedges against foreign currency economic exposures.

If you'd know the

Value of Money,

go and borrow some.

Benjamin Franklin,
Poor Richard's Almanac

Watch foreign governments . . . closely

As the crises in Asia and Latin America in the late 1990s illustrated, U.S. firms entering international business transactions need to be cautious of foreign governments. Many national governments over the years with a stated goal of a fixed exchange rate against the U.S. dollar have ultimately let their currencies float. Such changes in exchange rate policy have often hurt both local and foreign businesses. Thus, a U.S. firm going global needs to be wary of the economic and exchange rate policies of foreign governments.

The exchange rate between the currencies of two countries is generally determined in the foreign exchange market. Countries whose currencies float, such as the U.S. dollar, allow the exchange rate to vary minute by minute depending upon the supply and demand for the two currencies. A currency in high demand will tend to appreciate against other currencies, while a currency in low demand will tend to depreciate.

Many foreign governments have a tendency to intervene in foreign exchange markets, often with an eye to fix the exchange rate between their country's currency and another currency, say, the U.S. dollar, the Japanese yen, the German mark, or, in time, the Euro. The motivation of a foreign government for fixing the U.S. dollar value of its currency is the belief that a less volatile exchange rate will tend to encourage international trade. To achieve this stability, when a foreign currency is in high demand by market forces, tending to appreciate the currency, the foreign government's central bank increases the supply of its currency (by buying U.S. dollars and adding these to the nation's currency reserves). When a foreign currency is in low demand, tending to depreciate the currency, the foreign central bank decreases the supply of its currency (by selling U.S. dollars and thereby reducing its currency reserves).

Problems usually surface when the market generates a low demand for a country's currency. When a foreign country has accelerating inflation, growing national government budget deficits, or an increasing international trade deficit, foreign exchange traders start to expect the foreign currency to depreciate. The market has a low demand for the country's currency, and the value of the foreign currency should depreciate. However, foreign governments often attempt first to deplete their nation's currency reserves trying to defend the exchange rate. Often such defenses are overwhelmed by the speculative pressure of professional foreign exchange traders moving over a trillion dollars of currencies daily, and the foreign currency suffers a massive devaluation, as Brazil did in 1999.

U.S. managers doing business internationally need to closely monitor the exchange rates and macroeconomic policies in the foreign countries where they are doing business. The investment of time and resources into monitoring political and economic policies is a small insurance premium to pay to avoid large changes in exchange rates and relative prices that might disrupt dramatically an export or import business.

Is there an international code of business ethics?

Companies around the world are increasingly committing time and resources to better understand the ethical dimension of conducting business. This increased attention to the ethical implications of business decisions manifests itself in various ways. Large corporations have introduced ethical officers concerned with improving ethical behavior in corporate governance. Mission statements of several companies embrace sensitivity to ethical behavior, human conditions, and environmental responsibility. Corporations are establishing discussion groups, training sessions, and centers for business ethics.

In the United States, academic business ethicists have identified the growing awareness as more practically oriented or pragmatic. The statement "Good ethics is good business" suggests that being ethical in business decisions is efficient; that is, a U.S. business will prosper in the long run by not making myopic unethical decisions in the short run. One might interpret this particular

Do other men, for they would do you; that's the true business precept.

Charles Dickens

approach to business ethics as "value-free." However, this approach is consistent with an ethical approach founded upon the personal and religious values of individuals. A practice-oriented approach to business ethics—manifested most prominently in publicly touted ethical mission statements of U.S. corporations—has possibly allowed discussion of ethical standards among U.S. businesses to flourish in the past decade.

By contrast, ethical discussions in Europe tend to focus less upon the business organization and more upon underlying philosophical notions. Consequently, such discussions may reflect personal value judgments more. The discussions are inherently more difficult because ethical conversation is interwoven with language, and Europe lacks the common language of English used in U.S. dialogues. Because Europe tends to maintain stronger social policies than the United States, ethical discussions focus less on business and more on national policies. In yet other countries, national religious homogeneity has important implications for ethical considerations. Some business ethicists have argued against ethical comparisons across countries, due to differences influenced by various cultural and religious factors.

Observations such as these suggest that ethical standards are not universal. Ethical standards are interwoven with a country's business, religious, and sociological structure. There is likely no international code of business ethics because the standards are influenced so strongly by the nation's people and culture. Yet many established multinational corporations have adopted sets of standards with some common denominator applicable to the numerous markets served.

Ethical decisions for a U.S. firm consequently become even more difficult when made in a foreign business context. Just as language becomes a barrier to trade and implicitly an additional cost associated with an international transaction, differences internationally in ethical standards increase the cost of doing business overseas. Thus, the U.S. firm going global needs to research thoroughly the customs and culture of the foreign country being considered for a business transaction to maintain ethical integrity in the exchange. Since European business people are more accustomed to international differences than the typical U.S. manager, European firms have more experience with gauging ethical norms in foreign markets.

While an international code of business ethics likely does not yet exist, two important points are worth noting. First, countries individually are developing increasingly standards of ethical business decision consistent with prevailing cultural and business norms. For instance, the United States has long had a policy of eliminating corruption in business transactions. Recently, the Organization for Economic Cooperation and Development's (O.E.C.D.) agreement on Combating Bribery of Foreign Public Officials in International Business Transactions was signed to rid firms of corrupt business practices. Second, differences in ethical standards among countries are likely eroding. International travel, the Internet, exchanges of films, books, and periodicals will augment the sharing of information and tastes, creating a global environment for eliminating differences in ethical standards among businesses. Indeed, numerous established multinational corporations have certainly advanced the notion of global codes of conduct in business transactions.

Consult thoroughly public sources of trade information

The U.S. government provides extensive resources that can significantly aid a U.S. export or import business. The U.S. Department of Commerce provides considerable written material and human resources to help businesses select and enter a foreign market. State governments also actively counsel businesses on the nuances of foreign trade.

The U.S. Department of Commerce has long provided excellent materials for helping a business begin to export. The Department's *A Basic Guide to Exporting* is an excellent source for introductory information. The International Trade Administration, within the department, has a subdivision called the U.S. and Foreign Commercial Service. This section has a staff of officers in foreign cities to help U.S. exporters and importers. The Department of Commerce also maintains international trade specialists in its numerous district offices in major cities. District offices provide information on foreign markets, overseas buyers, financing opportunities, trade exhibitions, and export documentation counseling.

The Export Administration is another division within the U.S. Department of Commerce. The administration provides counseling in export controls and helps U.S. exporters comply with export laws and regulations.

The U.S. Department of State also provides assistance and counseling for potential U.S. exporters and importers. Within the State Department, the Bureau of Economic and Business Affairs handles most responsibilities on economic matters and the promotion of international trade. The bureau and department have extensive operations around the world to provide U.S. exporters with commercial assistance.

State commerce departments also provide excellent assistance for the U.S. business going global. Such departments offer educational material on exporting, organize trade missions to foreign markets, and help sponsor trade shows and exhibitions.

On the local level, most cities' Chambers of Commerce actively promote exporting. Chambers of Commerce promote seminars, trade shows, and overseas trade missions as part of their programs to help local businesses interested in expanding operations internationally.

Finally, the U.S. Customs Service provides information to potential U.S. importers of goods and services. The Customs Service's *Importing Into the United States* provides an excellent introduction to the business of importing.

It isn't the oceans
which cut us off from
the world — it's the
American way of
looking at things.

Henry Miller

INDEX

AUTHOR

JEFFREY H. BERGSTRAND, Ph.D., is an Associate Professor of Finance and Business Economics in the College of Business Administration at the University of Notre Dame. He has been teaching about the global macroeconomic environment and about international finance in the undergraduate, MBA, and executive MBA programs since 1986, earning Outstanding Teacher of the Year awards in both the MBA and Executive MBA programs. He has published numerous articles on exchange rates and international trade patterns for academic journals and currently coedits the *Review of International Economics*, an academic journal.